BLACK BEAR

by Daniel J. Cox

Introduction by Denny Olson
Foreword by Michael Furtman

Chronicle Books · San Francisco

Dedication

I dedicate this book to a very unique and special person, one who believed in my talent, desire, and enthusiasm long before I proved it to others. That special person is Jackson Huntley. With his intuitive guidance I began the journey that has taken many rewarding paths, one of them leading to this book. Thank you, Jackson. Also, as always, to my sweet and loving wife, Julie.

Photographs copyright © 1989 by Daniel J. Cox.

Printed in Japan

Library of Congress Cataloging-in-Publication Data

Cox. Daniel J., 1960–
    Black bear / Daniel J. Cox ; introduction by Denny Olson ;
foreword by Michael Furtman.
        p.   cm.
    ISBN 0-87701-727-1. — ISBN 0-87701-684-4 (pbk.)
    1. Black bear—Lake States.   2. Black bear—Lake States—
Pictorial works.   I. Title.
QL737.C27C68   1990
599.74'446—dc20   90-40768
                                                                        CIP

Book and cover design: Brenda Rae Eno

Distributed in Canada by Raincoast Books,
112 East Third Avenue, Vancouver, B.C. V5T 1C8

10 9 8 7 6 5 4 3 2 1

Chronicle Books
275 Fifth Street
San Francisco, California 94103

Title page: A young cub follows its mother into a meadow.

Foreword

DAN LOOKED LIKE HE NEEDED A CUP OF COF-fee. He stood in the door of his camper on the bed of his rusty and weary Toyota pickup. His hair was heaped wildly, his eyes still groggy from a night's sleep. "Do you have any coffee?" he groaned. I fetched a thermos from the cab of my truck.

I suppose most people believe that the life of a free-lance wildlife photographer is glamorous. Being employed in a similar field, outdoor writing, I can attest to the fact that there are moments of splendor when you realize that you get paid to enjoy yourself. There are also many hours and days of hard work with no guarantee of pay and a lot of time spent alone, away from loved ones, eating from tin cans and counting pennies.

I found Dan camped in a gravel pit in the northern Midwest woods, living a barebones existence and in dire need of caffeine. We had arranged an early-morning rendezvous at this spot so I could follow Dan to where he had been photographing the shy black bears of this dense northern forest. When he invited me, I jumped at the chance, curious to find out how he got close enough to the bears to complete his task of documenting their hidden lives on film. Much wildlife photography is done in the West or the Arctic where open landscapes and long lenses make capturing animals on film possible, if not easy. But photographing wildlife in the tangled jack-straw woodlands of this region is a different story.

Leaving the campsite, I drove behind Dan down twisting gravel roads to the area he had been working in. As he retrieved his camera gear from the camper, I wandered into a nearby clearing. Within moments a massive brown-phase black bear appeared, lumbering toward me from the bushes that had screened him. I froze.

"Don't move," called Dan. "Just put your hands palms forward so he can see you aren't holding anything."

Don't move! Of course I wouldn't move. I simply couldn't. My feet no longer received orders from my brain. I slowly raised my hands and held them, empty, before me.

The big bear stopped a couple of feet in front of me. I could see wood ticks on his ears and smell his breath. Taking one more step, he sniffed the camera hanging around my neck. He licked the lens. He moved his broad snout toward my crotch. I closed my eyes.

When I opened them, Dan was next to me. The bear had waddled across the clearing toward a small stream at the edge of the forest. Dan grabbed my arm and pulled me to follow him.

"He's a nice bear. You don't need to worry about him," he whispered. "Come on, maybe we'll get some shots of him at the creek."

To my amazement, Dan scurried to within a few yards of the bear and followed him into the woods. I stuck near Dan. With incredible stealth, the four-hundred-pound bear snaked through the dense brush, paying no attention at all to us.

So this was Dan's secret! He had gained the confi-dence of these animals. He had become so much a part

Above: Chokecherries are a favorite food of black bears. Though they are generally solitary animals, they will often tolerate the presence of other bears in a large berry patch.

of their daily existence that they no longer considered him a threat. Now I had been invited to join them. In a few short hours I began to see the world with a decidedly bruinish outlook and gained a perspective that changed my opinion of black bears forever.

The Ojibway Indians native to this region considered the bear their brother. Bears, they thought, were wise; though they did kill and eat black bears, they also revered them, imploring them to share their wisdom. The black bear was even the totem of their secret *midewewin* ("grand medicine") society. Sadly, what the Ojibway learned from the black bear is hidden or lost in the genocidal destruction of Ojibway culture.

Now Dan had become the brother of the black bear. With his respectful approach they allowed him to probe their secret ways, let him live with them through many hot, cold, wet, mosquito-infested miles and days. What I learned that day with Dan Cox, deep in the alder,

birch, and spruce forest of the north woods, is that these bruins are a peaceful lot, content to feed and sleep and play. Were they of bad humor, such powerful animals could be dangerous, but the side of them we saw only revealed an existence of contented wandering and scavenging.

Few are lucky enough to receive an invitation such as I did. Fewer still will get to know the black bear as has Dan. Fortunately for all of us, my friend Dan Cox has the skill and patience necessary to follow these bears and capture them in these wonderful photographs. Just as I followed on Dan's elbow that memorable day, let him guide you into the hidden world of the shy black bear.

MICHAEL FURTMAN

BEARS

by Denny Olson

MY FIRST BEAR EXPERIENCE BEGAN ONE WARM afternoon at a lakeside campsite. I had calmly reassured my group, "In leading fifteen years of canoe trips, I have never had a bear in camp." I explained to my group that poor cleanliness and inadequate food storage are the main reasons campers have bear problems. With these words, I ensured a bear visit that night.

Actually, what I said about inadequate food storage was true. Our overly tired crew hung "Galactapack," a behemoth Duluth pack full of bear delicacies, a little too close to the tree trunk on an overburdened branch. A minor risk, considering I had never had bear problems.

At 4:00 A.M. the distinctive sound of large claws on red-pine bark intruded on my smug sleep. "Naw." I rolled over. I heard the sound again. This time, I woke my co-leader and gave him the news in the matter-of-fact way of seasoned woodsmen.

"Bear!" I screamed in my softest whisper, not wanting to panic the group. We stumbled from the tent and began banging on pots and yelling at the top of our lungs. The group was sure that the Apocalypse had come.

The bear ignored us from its perch in the red pine. It slapped at the pack, leaning away from the trunk. The pack spun like a tetherball. This large bear looked to our stunned eyes like the 1200-pound version of its Kodiak Island relative, the brown bear. I moved toward it, still banging and yelling. The bear bounced lightly out of the

tree, took two hops in my direction, and popped its jaws, its ears back.

We retreated in a calm and orderly fashion. The bear went back to playing tetherball, while the campers practiced CPR and hyperventilation. Discretion seemed to call for surrender, but it was 4:00 A.M. and this was *my* food.

The nice thing about being half-asleep is that rational thoughts leave and instinct takes over. I grabbed a fencepost log and stomped three-legged toward the bear, growling and popping *my* jaws. My partner stayed behind, perfectly willing to let natural selection take its course, secure in the knowledge that if the bear ate me, it would be too full to eat *his* food.

The bear searched its memory banks for encounters with a three-legged blob and found none. New stimuli seemed to win in the dominance game—the bear leaped backwards into the brush and vanished. Having won that encounter, I stuck out my chest but secretly wondered how I could have been so stupid. My partner shrugged and went back to bed. The campers whispered in their tents until morning. For the rest of the week they watched me out of the corners of their eyes and did everything I asked, exactly and quickly.

We saw seven black bears on that trip, six black black and one brown. (The name *black bear* is an endless source of confusion, considering how varied the color range for the species is.) That year, one of the important crops of the bears' summer schedule, hazelnuts, was a dismal failure, and, being models of opportunism, they filled the gap with garbage and canoe packs. But not one human being was recruited for ursine sustenance, though the bears were extremely hungry and had thousands of encounters with campers. In fact, one of the world's experts on black bears has found himself positioned between females and cubs, supposedly the most dangerous of encounters, hundreds of times, without ever being attacked. Usually the mother will run off and pop her jaws from a healthy distance, while her cubs climb the nearest tree.

This expert also believes that human beings can nearly always back down a black bear. He advocates defending food caches. Allowing bears to eat their fill only teaches them to do it again; it also reinforces the message that human beings are pushovers to mild intimidation. (My lawyer, of course, would disagree with encouraging readers to confront bears.)

I'm not saying bear attacks are impossible. Black bears kill a person every thirty years or so, and there were two attacks by the same bear in Minnesota's boundary waters a couple of years ago. The expert researcher I just cited had his shirt ripped wide open by a swipe from the only bear whose behavior was an exception to the usual confrontation. Black bears get their fierce reputation from their cousins, the grizzly bear. Most black bears, however, will do almost anything to avoid a confrontation with even the shyest of individuals.

What bears really do well is mind their own business, eat, and sleep. Northern Midwest bears have female-only territoriality, and their territories average seven square miles. Males range wherever their appetites take them. All summer, they are in a state of hyperphagia, which is a biological camouflage word for overeating. Later, during the cold half of the year, they become anorexic. It all balances out. Bears are models of opportunism, switching from fresh aspen leaves to ant colonies to the berry *du jour*, and they almost always have the switches timed perfectly. They fill the gaps with garbage, Purina Dog Chow, and canoeing packs, when available.

In the Northern Midwest canoe country, sarsaparilla, hazelnuts, and insects are typical fare. Across the rest of the continent, the menu includes more species than it excludes. Autumn acorns often represent the last chance for building fat reserves, and bears will often travel fifty miles to get them. By October bears migrate back toward their home ranges. On the way home, life slows down considerably, and they phase into hibernation. By the time they enter their dens, they have been in a state of walking hibernation for two weeks.

When do bears finally dive into their dens? Most researchers feel that the first snow, temperature changes, atmospheric pressure, and photoperiod all have something to do with the timing. Hibernation occurs regardless of food availability. The current hypothesis says that reduced thyroid gland activity, triggered by the amount of body fat, is the final incentive.

Textbooks remind us that bears are not true hibernators, in tones reserved for the second-rate castes of this world. True hibernators, such as ground squirrels, are studied with an air of reverence. True hibernators shut down to 10 percent of their normal metabolic rates, while heart and breathing rates become almost nonexistent. The mystical "brown fat" of true hibernators stays liquid at temperatures far below freezing. Science looks at true hibernators with awe. After all, it can't explain the process yet.

Bears drop their body temperature about 10 degrees. Their heart and breathing rates drop only slightly. But unlike chipmunks, bears give birth and nurse cubs during hibernation. Once asleep, bears are energy conservationists and recyclers that would shame any environmentalist. For five months they don't move from their chambers. They use only fat for energy, not protein like true hibernators. Nor do they urinate or defecate, like true hibernators. Bears reprocess urea from the urine back into muscle tissue, and they actually *gain* muscle mass over the winter.

While asleep, they lose 20 to 40 percent of their weight, all fat. In the process they actually produce an acid that dissolves gallstones, a problem often experienced by human beings on starvation diets. Modern medicine has taken notice: bear acid extract is the remedy of choice for gallstones.

Sows are fertile anytime from May to September, and mating is a matter of convenience. From this, it would seem logical for cubs to be born over a wide range of dates. Not so. Female bears use delayed implantation, meaning that the fertilized egg does not begin to grow until it implants itself in the uterine wall, usually at denning time. The result is that most cubs are born in mid-January, ensuring that most of their nursing will be done on a sleeping mother. The precision of this timing suggests that implantation is photoperiod-controlled—an ursine decoding of the astronomical clock.

Pregnant females are the first bears to enter dens in the fall and the last to leave in the spring. You might think that pregnant sows would want to carry cubs internally through a cold winter, but it makes more sense for them to do pregnancy externally. Young bears would be severely stressed by toxin levels inside a mother who recycles everything for five months. The solution? Escape the womb early, stay close to a mother just warm enough to keep the cubs warm too, drink high-fat milk

(33 percent compared to 3 percent in human beings), and wait for spring. The sows eat their cubs' feces and reprocess the droppings into milk and protein.

Cubs are born naked, the size of squirrels, with large heads and front feet. After a week or so they get their first black hair. At six weeks their eyes open, and at three months they get their permanent teeth. They stay with their mother throughout their first year and finally get booted out the following spring. This means, of course, that females only mate every two years. Combine that low reproduction potential with the slow maturation rate of bears (females and males reach sexual maturity at five and six years, respectively), and there is good reason to show caution setting hunting quotas.

When bears emerge in the spring, they are not ravenous, as you might expect. For about three weeks, they eat very little and seldom urinate as their body chemistry readjusts after five months of hibernation.

Bears are models of pragmatism. They often resemble Cuisinarts in their ability to process food nonstop. Legends of camp-robbing bears dwell on their ingenuity at extracting packs from campers with the least effort. But when the winter wind is howling and the country lies still and white, bears are at their best.

Although bears in modern times are often considered a nuisance, it hasn't always been that way. To traditional native Americans, bears are animals of incredible power and insight. They are the animals of introspection. Because bears are nearsighted, nocturnal, and spend all winter in a den, their ability to see the world around them is limited. But perhaps when they look within themselves they see a landscape as varied and beautiful as the outer one. Bears have no trouble navigating their country, and that is only a mystery to us when we don't see them as teachers. Perhaps our knowledge of the land is there inside us, too. From the bear, we may someday learn to look deeply enough.

Above: Bears are very much at home in trees. Cubs learn quickly upon leaving the den that their long claws are their main defense, allowing them to climb trees to elude predators.

Next page: A hot summer day drives the bears into the murky waters of the swamp. Besides the heat, deer flies and mosquitoes also make summer a miserable time for bears.

SPRING

LIFE IN THE NORTHERN MIDWEST WOODS HAD begun to thaw. Winter had blanketed the land for over seven months and it was now time for the warmth of spring to awaken life and allow the waters to run, the birds to return, and arctic highs to retreat. Soon the mother black bear would emerge from her winter den with her four tiny cubs to begin life above ground for another year.

Time passed lazily as I scouted the familiar cedar bogs and surrounding highlands. I knew from other years that spring is a time when bears are in short supply. It takes a month or two before they return from the great distances they traveled the autumn before. The Department of Natural Resources has used radio collars to keep close tabs on a number of black bears over the years. They have discovered that some bears hibernate well over a hundred miles from where they spend their summers. But this bountiful area, rich with food, calls them back. With some bears denning nearer this area than others, I thought my chances of meeting one were very good.

You might think bears would be easy to find. They are big and seem heavy enough to crack twigs and break brush, making a great deal of noise when they travel. Amazingly, that's not the case. Even in this area, with its high concentration of black bears, finding one when it doesn't want to be found is very difficult. Bears are extremely quiet most of the time, so quiet it can be spooky. I've lost count of the times I've followed a bear a scant twenty to twenty-five feet back, only to have it duck behind a blowdown and, before I could regain eye contact, vanish. No sound, no movement, not a noise to be heard as I scanned the black spruce and cedar groves.

Evening shadows began to envelop the densely forested north woods, obscuring any light for photography. The day was ending and so I decided to return to the road and my camper. On the grassy old logging trail, I finally met her. Off in the distance, at fifty yards, stood a very large bear. Her polished coat glistened as she sniffed the air, head swaying from side to side as she glanced in my direction. I heard a slight *woof*. The grass behind her divided in many different directions. As she stepped forward for a better look, my body tensed. I heard a flurry of claws rake into the aspen tree at the edge of the trail. Up out of the grass, clinging to the trunk, scampered four balls of black. She *woofed* again and swatted the ground in front of her, lunging and popping her jaws to intimidate me. Once the cubs were high in the tree, she rushed to the trunk and followed them up. There in the branches clung a family of five. More grunts, whines, *woofs* and blowing created a major commotion in the upper branches of the aspen.

I watched for a moment and then picked a route out of there, skirting, for safety, the logging road and the tree the bears claimed. In my three years of photographing black bears and dozens of encounters with sows and cubs, never once have any females carried out the impressive threats they have so often displayed. With the sow in the tree, I knew my chances of being harmed were very slim, but even so I showed my respect by picking a route she wouldn't think threatening. Down the trail I hiked, heart pounding and feeling exhilarated! The sun dropped behind the aspens and the shadows lengthened. It was the start of another great year in the land of the black bear.

Opposite page: A very young cub struggles to pull itself over a fallen log. Its extremely sharp claws were well developed before leaving the winter den. Those claws allow it to climb trees with the blazing speed that is its main defense against potential predators, including the adult male black bear.

Below: A sow curls tightly into a ball to help protect her cubs from the winter's cold. Entering the den in the fall, the sow built the grass nest they now rest on. The den is very clean and smells like hay. This particular den (left) is beneath a sparsely covered brush pile that offers almost no protection from the frigid winter temperatures.

Above: A young cub stays close to its mother. Their relationship will last for nearly two years.

Above: A young cub displays the typical erect-stance posture of bears when they want to get a better look at something or test the wind for scent.

Above, top: A sow and her cubs rest in a lush meadow.
Above: A pair of young cubs explores the grasses for ants, grasshoppers, or anything else that may be edible.

Above, top: A lone cub braves the meadow, leaving the safety of a tree to follow its mother.
Above: A cub, standing for a better look, finds comfort in leaning against its mother. Though black bear sows are very protective, they are not as ferocious and unpredictable as their relatives, the grizzly bears.

Previous page: A lone bear searches for white suckers on the banks of a spring stream.

Left: Like their relatives, the grizzly bears, black bears enjoy a meal of fish. Late spring brings spawning white suckers to the northern streams. The bears scavenge the banks and wade the streams searching for a high-protein meal.

Above: A cinnamon-colored cub chases after his black sibling, hoping to steal his playmate's fish. White suckers from the creek are a late-spring delicacy, and these two cubs have no intentions of sharing.
Left: A yearling cub feeds on a white sucker.

Previous page: A cinnamon-colored yearling cub dashes towards its mother. Cinnamon is one of the many different colors of black bears; others include black, blonde, reddish or chocolate brown. A black sow often produces cubs of different colors.

Left and above: Yearling cubs play a game in the limbs of an aspen tree. The cub nearest the trunk will not let the other cub pass by, cutting off its escape. In their tussles, one of the cubs slips and nearly falls. Hanging from the branch, it tries to gain control and pull itself up.

Above: A yearling cub reaches up to grab a tree. Adult bears have been observed making similar motions. Some researchers believe this may be a type of scent-marking technique.

Above: A yearling cub plays with a sapling, using it to scratch its back. This behavior may be a form of scent marking.

Above: Black bears are omnivores, meaning they will eat practically anything. Here, a male bear has found the decaying carcass of a stillborn whitetail fawn. Even though their diet is mainly plant matter, bears relish a high-protein meal of meat when they can find it.

Left: Two siblings, just over a year old, tussle with each other at the edge of the cedar swamp.

Above: A sow and cub pause in the swamp for a little affection. The cub's eyes are surrounded by wood ticks.

Above: A bear pauses to scratch. Over twenty different species of parasites, including ticks, lice, and fleas, are known to infect black bears.

Above: The muddy water of a swamp slakes this bear's thirst. Bears cross the swamp frequently at this location, using the log as a bridge.

SUMMER

The land was saturated in lush green. The season had rolled into summer, bringing unbearably hot temperatures that enveloped the swamp, evaporating the water into sheets of invisible moisture that drenched everything. The swamp buzzed with the activity of pesky insects too numerous to count. Vegetation was so thick that at times I had to crawl to my destination, swatting bugs and detouring around waterholes. There I sat, looking up through this maze of green, waiting and watching my subject, a sleeping bear. My perch was a patch of higher ground maybe three inches above the soggy moss-covered floor of the cedar swamp. I leaned against the willow branches that sprouted from the clump of trees I had hoped would keep me dry. I was miserable.

My mind wandered back to the day's beginning. Nearly two hours before, I had arrived at a clearing and found my willing subject. He was one of the larger bears I had been photographing. I found him leisurely grazing on the saturated grasses that grew in the meadow. I retrieved my cameras and began to approach him, taking photos as I progressed. I hoped this would be the day I had been waiting for. One that would take me to the blueberry patches, for I knew from the bear scat I was finding that the berries had ripened and bears were feeding on them.

Off I went, following my acquaintance. At first the going was fairly easy; the trails that had been made over many years offered easy walking. However, after only a half-mile or so, the swamp began to close in. I'm never surprised to see how well adapted these animals are to getting through their environment. Wildlife photography teaches you that animals are amazingly adept and well suited to the environments they live in. But we have a harder time traveling where bears go. Carrying twenty-five pounds of photo gear makes the going even tougher. Up and over, down and across, switching the tripod from right to left shoulder, grabbing a branch while using a fallen tree as a bridge, all the while doing your best to keep your eyes on an animal that can disappear in the blink of an eye.

The hike led me deeper and deeper into the swamp. We crossed two rivers, rivers that looked more like ponds than moving water. The bear used a crisscross of fallen trees to span the muddy ponds. Not having claws to grip the wet, slimy surface of the fallen trees, I ended up wading. My fourteen-inch L. L. Bean boots, which I could usually count on for miracles, were no match for the flooded trails. On I trudged, while the bear glided effortlessly from dry spot to dry spot.

Finally, the swamp receded. The lowland vegetation opened up to higher ground and an expanse of young aspens. Here I stood, watching the bear dig into a rotting log. A few quick tugs and the log split apart. Ants spilled out, scurrying everywhere while the bear's tongue darted towards its miniature prey. Moments passed, then on he went, heading directly for a clearcut where blueberries grew in profusion. My excitement lasted only briefly, for the bear showed no interest in the berries. He skirted the clearing and headed for a stand

of thick willows, a buffer between the clearcut and the river. Lowering his head, he ducked down a trail and sauntered into the brush for another twenty-five feet. There, next to a stump, the bear lay down and slumbered.

For the next four hours, there I sat. Lush green in every direction, patches of blue in the far distance. My legs were soaked to the thighs, and sweat poured down my back and stomach. Mosquitoes and deer flies buzzed in circles around my head, ravenous for the easy meal a

man provides. No breakfast before I left; for now, no lunch while I waited. I was starved and the trip back was long and hard. I still hoped the bear would wake and visit the blueberry patch, so I stuck it out. At any moment, my luck might change and I would get my blueberry-eating black bear pictures. Hours passed. Finally I went to the berry patch myself to squelch the knots forming in my stomach. Early evening was approaching. Soon I would have to leave, for there was no way I could return in the dark.

Left: A bear pauses to sniff the air on a dew-soaked morning. Insects of all kinds make up a portion of a bear's diet. However, the spider that made this web will probably go unnoticed by the bear.

Suddenly the bear got up, headed for the river, now wider and much deeper, slid into the cool tea-colored water, and swam to the other side. I could only watch. I could not cross with my gear. Within seconds, he was out of sight. I watched in disappointment. There would be another day, but now it was time to head back. I took a compass reading and turned east.

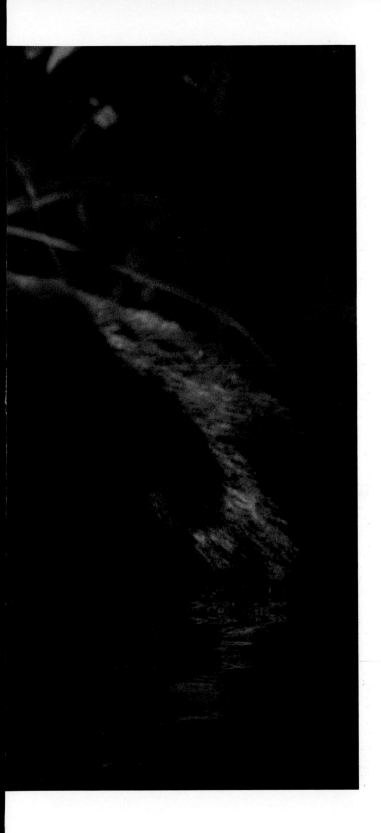

Left: A large male cools himself in the tea-colored swamp waters. Temperatures in the north woods can reach 95° in the summer.

Above: Being omnivores, bears are usually near something they can eat. They are extremely opportunistic and will eat food whenever it's available. This bear, soaking in cool water to escape the summer heat, takes a bite from a bush along a stream bank.

Above: The lush, tangled habitat of black bears is the major reason why they are so seldom seen.

Above: With lightning speed, a cub bolts up an aspen tree to safety. An adult male, if given the chance, will sometimes go after cubs.

Opposite page: A cinnamon sow and her three cubs take refuge in an aspen tree. When the threat of danger is severe, the sow will follow her cubs into the tree and stay with them until she feels the threat is gone.

Previous page: A large aspen provides a comfortable and safe spot for a napping bear. A drenching rain seems to have no effect on the bear's disposition.

Above: Swollen waters from a summer rain cover a favorite trail. To get from one side to the other, a sow leaps over the creek.

Left: An adult male pauses while feeding on highbush blueberries.

Below and right: A yearling cub (right) and a young sow (below) feed on the leaves of a beaked hazel bush. During August the hazel bushes produce large nuts (above) that are a favorite food of many woodland creatures. The bears are no exception.

Above: Hearing the approach of another bear, this family stands erect, trying to get a better view. Because cubs are vulnerable to predation by adult males, the sow stays alert, ready to order the cubs up a tree.

Above: Alert, a young cub stands on its hind legs. Approximately five pounds upon leaving the den, cubs can weigh nearly thirty pounds by midsummer. A varied diet of fruits, herbs, carrion, and grass allows them to grow strong.

Above and opposite page: A cinnamon-colored sow attacks a male black bear. The sow still has her cubs from the year before and is not ready to breed with the male. His advances are too early; it will be another two weeks before she runs her cubs off and is ready to breed again. Until then she is fiercely protective and sees any male bear as a threat to the lives of her cubs.

Above: A young cub escapes danger by climbing a tree.
Left: A large bear pauses in the tall grass of late summer.

Left: A young bear pauses for a drink at streamside on a hot summer day.

Above: A male bear finds a receptive sow and is permitted to mate with her. Bears were once thought to be monogamous on a year-to-year basis. However, this male was also photographed mating with a different sow. The bears' breeding season begins in June and ends around the first week of July. This mating lasted about forty-five minutes. A sow will be fertile until she is approximately twenty years old.

Left and Above: A sow and her cubs spend the middle part of the day deep within the forest. The female rests with her cubs and will order them up a tree should danger approach. The standing cub is picking wood ticks from its mother's ears.

Sibling cubs wrestle with each other
on a regular basis.

AUTUMN TO WINTER

THE ACTIVITY OF THE SPRING AND SUMMER WAS coming to an end. The colors of the land had changed from bright greens to shimmering reds and yellows. Blue skies gave way to slate gray clouds that floated just above the tips of the spruce and cedars. The berries were gone and, soon, the bears would go too. Autumn had arrived.

Once again I found myself tramping the woods, searching for a subject. As in the spring, however, the bears were scarce and so I found myself wandering, looking for anything of interest to view through my lens. In a chance meeting, a yearling bear from last season's brood walked through the meadow. I changed my course to his and followed, spending the morning with him before he decided to part company with me.

With autumn's cool nights and changing colors, the bears seem to realize that it is time to find a den for the next five months. It's amazing what a bear will choose for winter hibernation. Though the word *den* conjures up a warm, snug, and comfortable hole underground, many dens are not like that at all. The hibernaculum, or bedroom, can be just about anything, depending on the bear. I once found a large, snow-covered bear sleeping at the base of a large pine. Another den I found was a nicely shaped round hole dug into a sandy bank. A tunnel of several feet led inside. There, at the back, slept a sow and her three month-old cubs on a nest of grasses.

Sows will usually search for a better den than boars will, at least in my experience. One winter, however, I was led to the den of a female with cubs. It was in the middle of a recently logged area. Slashings, brush piles,

and natural debris were scattered over the open ground. Aspens the size of my thumb stretched through the snow, working to make another forest. In one of these brush piles, an acquaintance of mine had found a sow sleeping through the winter.

Her winter shelter was an excellent den for photography because it was nearly open on top. However, what's good for pictures is not necessarily good for a long winter's nap, especially with babies to care for. How the cubs survived in such an open structure I couldn't understand. A few weeks earlier, the temperature had reached 30 degrees below zero. Gaping holes in the roof of this brush pile allowed any heat that was produced to escape. Not only did it seem that the cubs might freeze, but being very vocal they would be easy to hear. There aren't many predators a bear has to worry about, but wolves are one. There were many in this area. The purring, suckling, and squalling cubs would easily give away their location. So far, they seemed to be doing fine.

It's possible to spook a bear from its winter sleep. (Even though they are very drowsy, they still are aware of something unusual happening.) I took my photos as quickly and unobtrusively as possible. It would be certain death for the cubs if the sow were scared from her den. I left quietly and hoped the family would survive the next month or so until they were ready for the warming months of spring. Here they would stay, the cubs nestled into the thick black fur of their mother, growing every day, waiting for her to waken and lead them into the melting snows of the outer world.

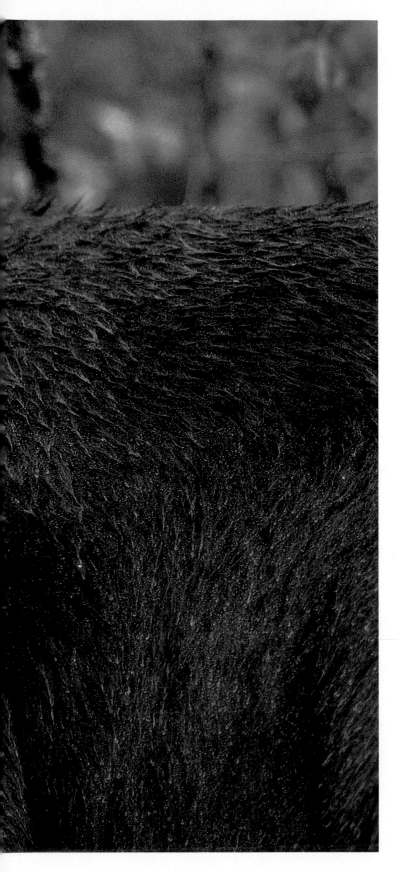

Previous page: A male pauses in the steamy bog, resting momentarily while foraging.

Left: A large male naps at the base of a cedar tree in the pouring rain.

Opposite page and above: The diet of black bears contains a large number of insects. Here, a male pulls over a rotted tree. After getting it down, he searches for the ants living inside.

Above and opposite page: A sow and her cubs forage for food. The cubs, nearly the size of their mother, will go to the den with her and will spend one more winter as a family unit. The cubs will be driven away next summer.

Previous page: A large male wakes up from his nap in a cedar swamp.

Above: An extremely well-fed, fat yearling cub sits near a mountain ash it is feeding on. The cub will live off this fat during its long winter sleep.

Opposite page: A yearling cub finds the fruit of a mountain ash. Relaxing, it pulls the bush down and delicately picks the berries.

Previous page: A male nimbly picks berries from a mountain ash. Bears usually don't take the time to be so delicate and will often strip fruit from a branch, leaves and all.

Left: A yearling cub pulls over a mountain ash tree to get at the bright red fruit.

Above: A large male pauses at the edge of a drained beaver pond on his daily routine of foraging for food.
Next page: A male, fat from a season's foraging, wanders through a thick cedar swamp. Frost predicts winter's arrival; the bear will spend the next five to six months in a deep sleep, living off the four-inch layer of fat he has accumulated.

Left: After a season of foraging, a large male rests in a cedar swamp. Snow will be coming soon and he will leave to find a den for the winter.

Above: A large male searches for food along the banks of a beaver pond.

Above: Bears frequently use the same trails year after year, in familiar areas. Here, a large male follows a trail through the forest.

Left and next page: A large male rests beneath a cedar tree. Winter hibernation is near.